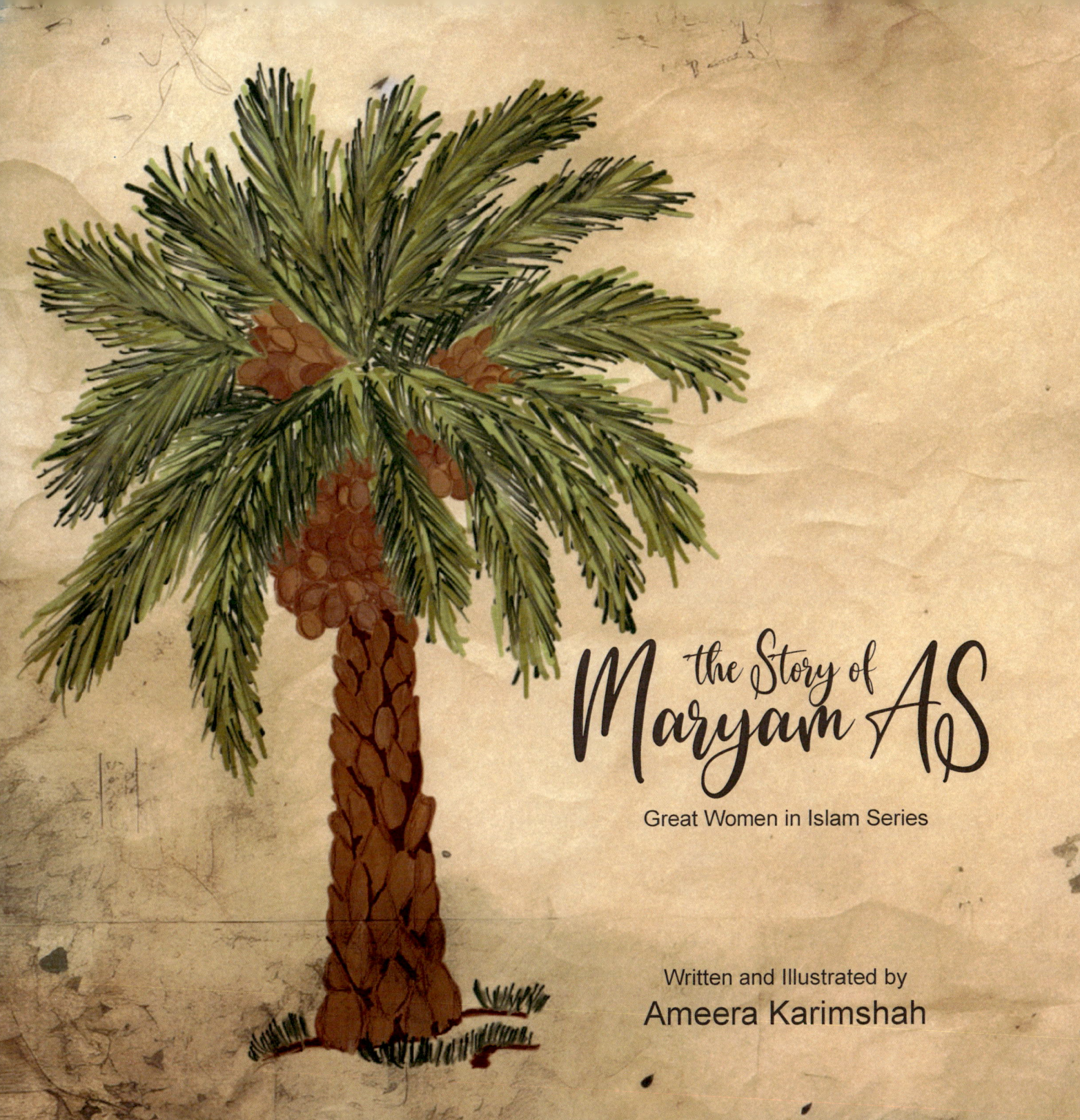

the Story of Maryam AS

Great Women in Islam Series

Written and Illustrated by
Ameera Karimshah

This is the story of Maryam (A.S) - daughter of Imran and Hannah.

Jerusalem Salvia
(Salvia Hierosolymitana)

She was among the truest believers in Allah and is given the highest honour in the Quran.

When Hannah was pregnant with Maryam (A.S) she made this dua:

"My lord, Certainly I have dedicated what is growing in my womb entirely to you, so accept this from me."

Allah accepted Hannah's dua and made Maryam (A.S) grow in goodness.
She devoted her whole life to praying to Allah.

Carob Tree
(Ceratonia siliqua)

Her father died before she was born, and so The Prophet Zakariyyah (A.S) was given the responsibility of raising Maryam (A.S).

Zakariyyah (A.S) was amazed and inspired by Maryam's (A.S) devotion to Allah (SWT).

Mountain Gazelle (Gazella Gazella)

When ever Zakariyyah (A.S) would visit her, she always had food with her.

He asked her where it was from and she replied "It is from near Allah. Certainly Allah provides for whoever he wills without explanation"

The angels visited Maryam (A.S) on many occasions and told her that she had been chosen Allah above all the women of the world.

White-spectacled bulbul
(Pycnonotus xanthopygos)

One day an angel appeared and told her she would give birth to a boy called Isa (A.S) and he would be amongst those nearest to Allah.

Maryam (A.S) asked Allah how she could have a child who had no father

The angel told her "That is how Allah is. He creates what he wills"

When it was time for Maryam (A.S) to have her baby she left the city and went to a remote place.

She was scared and in a lot of pain but Allah provided dates and water to comfort her and give her strength.

Allah (SWT) continued to protect Maryam after Isa (A.S) was born.

Mediterranean house gecko
(Hemidactylus turcicus)

He knew that people would think badly of Maryam (A.S) when she returned to the city with a baby so He told her to take a vow of silence and not speak to anyone.

Instead when people asked her about the child she just pointed to him.

Mediterranean fritillary (Argynnis pandora)

The miracle and blessing Allah granted Maryam (A.S) was giving her a baby that was able to speak! When the people said, "How can we speak to one who is in the cradle?"

Baby Isa (A.S) said "Certainly, I am the slave of Allah. He has given me the book and made me a prophet and he has made me blessed where ever I am"

Jeruselem Oak Goosefoot (Dysphania botrys)

And from that day on, everyone understood the truth. Maryam (A.S) was honoured as the mother of one of the greatest Prophets, and her courage and trust in Allah filled hearts everywhere with hope.

Her story shines like a bright star, reminding children and grown-ups alike that she is one of the finest role models the world has ever known.

ISBN 978-1-7637973-5-2
First Printed in 2026
©Copyright 1000 Tales

All rights reserved.
This book or any portion thereof may not be reproduced, stored in or introduced in a retrieval system, or transmitted, in any form or by any means without the express written permission of 1000 Tales except for the use of brief quotations in a book review.

Story and Illustrations by
Ameera Karimshah

We would like to acknowledge the Traditional Custodians of the continent of Australia. Whose cultures are among the oldest living cultures in human history and whose languages and knowledge have infused and inhabited this land for millennia.

We recognise their continuing connection to the land, waters and culture and we pay our respects to their Elders past, present and emerging.

www.ingramcontent.com/pod-product-compliance
Lightning Source LLC
Chambersburg PA
CBRC091503220426
43661CB00021B/1303